MW01716706

Your No. 1 Prayer Book To Learn To Be A Strong Christian Prayer Warrior That Prays With Powerful Prayers In The War Room To Overcome And Defeat The Enemy

Baltimore, Maryland

ACDAINC.ORG

Disclaimer

This book is a guide to help you strengthen your prayer life – it is not intended to guarantee that God will answer your prayers. Often times when God doesn't answer our prayers it is in fact an answer to prayers. Yet not too many of us realize this reality, we feel if God doesn't answer our prayers something's wrong and we often question – why? The truth of the matter is we may never know the why here on this side of heaven, but rest in the promises of God for He is faithful and just to take you from glory to glory and that He will direct your steps along the way as you continue to pray. God does not forsake His children but at times chastises them much like a tree in need of pruning. It doesn't always feel good and it's not always pleasant but most assuredly we know we can trust in God no matter what.

Unfortunately in today's society I have to put this disclaimer in this book so everyone has a clear understanding that I make no promise, guarantee, or assurance whether directly or indirectly that God will answer any of your prayers – that is completely and totally at the sole discretion of Almighty God, the Alpha and Omega, the great I am.

Furthermore it should be completely understood as previously mentioned that often times when we pray and we don't see God answering our prayers God is in fact answering our prayers for He knows the things that you have need of even before you ask. This is a critical concept to understand for we may pray an error or contrary to God's will for life but thanks be to God who leads us and guides us despite our ignorance.

Special Request

Thank you for purchasing our book and supporting our Ministry. We have a Special Request for those that have purchased this book on the Kindle platform. We wanted to make you aware that Amazon's Kindle platform pays per pages "read". Our Special Request is that if you appreciate our Ministry's efforts to put out books such as this or if you would simply like to support our Ministry's work to please scroll to the back of the book, even if you don't "read" the book right away. This is how we will get paid through the paid per pages criteria.

We all lead such busy lives nowadays and can get side tracked so easily please take a moment to support us now by allowing us to be paid by scrolling to the end of the book – Then go back and read it at your leisure. We deeply appreciate Your support and know that God will Bless You as You have Blessed this Ministry.

Dedication

This Book is dedicated to My Mom

~May You Rest in Peace (May 25, 1950 – November 10, 2016)~

This Book is Also Dedicated to Every Prayer Warrior Out there who Continues to Stand in the Gap and Pray for those Around them – God Bless You.

Forward

Prayer, along with the written Word (the Bible) is the most valuable tool we have when it comes to formulating a personal relationship with The Lord. The reason these two things are so essential can be summed up in one word—communication. It not only allows us to hear God, but communication is a two-way street. And prayer is the 'street' that allows us to communicate back to God.

Prayer is also the most misused, misunderstood, and un-used resource we have available to us. God created us in His image. His image! Do you understand what that means? It means we are as like God as any aspect of creation can be. It means we are special. It means God very much desires to have a relationship with us—one that is deeply personal. It means He will listen and answer our prayers when we pray because of His desire to be close to us.

You don't ignore your spouse, your children, your friends, or your boss when they talk to you, do you? Of course not! You also expect them to listen to you when you have something to say. So why do you think it should be any different with God? The answer to that question is this: It shouldn't be. Your willingness to talk to God and to have Him talk to you should be even greater than it is with the other relationships you have in your life.

The purpose of this book is to help you achieve that goal. By looking at what prayer is, how to pray, what to pray for, and when to pray, you will hopefully become more equipped and fully aware of what it means to pray to God and overcome and defeat the spiritual enemy.

Table of Contents

Chapter 1: What is Prayer?

Prayer is conversation between you and God. It is both speaking and listening. You speak. God listens. God speaks. You listen.

You speak

Prayer is the time you spend talking to God about the cares and concerns of your heart. It is the time you tell Him the desires of your heart. It is time spent praising God for being His amazing, holy, and wonderful self. It is time spent confessing your sins and asking God's forgiveness. It is time spent talking to God on behalf of family, friends, your church, our government, our military, missionaries, and whoever or whatever else concerns you.

God listens

God listens to each and every word we say. He even listens to our thoughts. Philippians 4:6 says, *Be careful for nothing; but in every thing by prayer and supplication with thanksgiving let your requests be made known unto God.* Did you get that? We can (and should) go to God about everything.

God listened to Elijah when he questioned God's decision to allow the widow's son to die. Once more, God gave Elijah what he asked for: *And he cried unto the Lord, and said, O Lord my God, hast thou also brought evil upon the widow with whom I sojourn, by slaying her son? And he stretched himself upon the child three times, and cried unto the Lord, and said, O Lord my God, I pray thee, let this child's soul come into him again. And the Lord heard the voice of Elijah; and the soul of the child came into him again, and he revived. (1st Kings 17:20-22)*

God listened to Mordecai when he prayed that God would intervene and save the Jewish race from annihilation at the hand of Haman (Esther4:1).

God listened to David when he asked God to forgive him for his sins of adultery and conspiracy for murder. David's prayer asking forgiveness is one of the most beautiful of all the psalms…

Have mercy upon me, O God, according to thy lovingkindness: according unto the multitude of thy tender mercies blot out my transgressions. Wash me throughly from mine iniquity, and cleanse me from my sin. For I acknowledge my transgressions: and my sin is ever before me. Against thee, thee only, have I sinned, and done this evil in thy sight: that thou mightest be justified when thou speakest, and be clear when thou judgest...

Purge me with hyssop, and I shall be clean: wash me, and I shall be whiter than snow. Make me to hear joy and gladness; that the bones which thou hast broken may rejoice. Hide thy face from my sins, and blot out all mine iniquities. Create in me a clean heart, O God; and renew a right spirit within me. Cast me not away from thy presence; and take not thy holy spirit from me. Restore unto me the joy of thy salvation; and uphold me with thy free spirit. (Psalm 51:1-4 and 7-12)

God listened to Jesus when He asked God to forgive those who were responsible for His death when He said, "*Then said Jesus, Father, forgive them; for they know not what they do." (Luke 23:34)*

God speaks

When we pray, we're not the only ones doing the talking. God does plenty of talking when we pray. No, we don't audibly hear God's voice like Abraham, Moses, Jonah, and numerous others did normally. But we hear God in that little voice that speaks to our heart and to our mind; telling us to do what we know is right and good. God's voice is the voice that warns us against sin and encourages us to go in the direction He created us to go.

Abraham's servant prayed to God; asking Him to provide the right woman for him to take home for Isaac to marry…

And he said O Lord God of my master Abraham, I pray thee, send me good speed this day, and shew kindness unto my master Abraham. Behold, I stand here by the well of water; and the daughters of the men of the city come out to draw water: And let it come to pass, that the damsel to whom I shall say,

Let down thy pitcher, I pray thee, that I may drink; and she shall say, Drink, and I will give thy camels drink also: let the same be she that thou hast appointed for thy servant Isaac; and thereby shall I know that thou hast shewed kindness unto my master. (Genesis 24:12-14)

God spoke to this man by giving him exactly what he asked for—a clear and definite answer as to the girl he was to take home to Isaac.

God audibly spoke to Moses countless times. One that especially stands out in my mind was the time God was so angry at the Israelites for building the golden calf and worshipping it that He told Moses He was going to kill them all and start over—creating a nation of people from Moses rather than Abraham. Let's look at this incident and then talk about it some more…

And the Lord said unto Moses, Go, get thee down; for thy people, which thou broughtest out of the land of Egypt, have corrupted themselves: They have turned aside quickly out of the way which I commanded them: they have made them a molten calf, and have worshipped it, and have sacrificed thereunto, and said, These be thy gods, O Israel, which have brought thee up out of the land of Egypt. And the Lord said unto Moses, I have seen this people, and, behold, it is a stiffnecked people: Now therefore let me alone, that my wrath may wax hot against them, and that I may consume them: and I will make of thee a great nation. And Moses besought the Lord his God, and said, Lord, why doth thy wrath wax hot against thy people, which thou hast brought forth out of the land of Egypt with great power, and with a mighty hand? Wherefore should the Egyptians speak, and say, For mischief did he bring them out, to slay them in the mountains, and to consume them from the face of the earth?

Turn from thy fierce wrath, and repent of this evil against thy people. Remember Abraham, Isaac, and Israel, thy servants, to whom thou swarest by thine own self, and saidst unto them, I will multiply your seed as the stars of heaven, and all this land that I have spoken of will I give unto your seed, and they shall inherit it for ever. And the Lord repented of the evil which he thought to do unto his people. (Exodus 2:7-14)

Some might say this wasn't actually a prayer, but considering the fact that prayer is conversation between us and God, I'd say it most definitely was. Keeping that in mind, let's take a more in-depth look at what God was *saying* to Moses in this brief encounter:

- God is instructing Moses; telling him to go down to the people.
- God is voicing his anger and hurt because Israel was so quick to turn their backs on God.

- It would have been or at least tempting (to some degree) for Moses to say, "Go ahead! Wipe them out and make me the new root of your people." But Moses didn't do that. Moses once again proved himself to be the humble servant of God he was. He reminded God of the promise He made to Abraham and telling God that he was trusting in Him to keep that promise.
- God voiced his pleasure with Moses in being so faithful and humble. He then did just what He had promised Abraham and allowed the Israelites to live.

God spoke to Paul when He didn't give Paul what he asked for—to take away whatever chronic ailment (thorn in the flesh) Paul was dealing with.

He wanted Paul to understand that he could be just as effective (if not more so) in the ministry with the ailment as he could without it. God wanted Paul to remember that the work he was doing was *through* him (Paul) *by* God.

FYI: God wants us to know the same.

You listen

The listening part of prayer on our part can be summed up in one word. Obedience.

Jonah didn't listen to God and paid a pretty steep price for his disobedience (Jonah 1). In spite of Jonah's disobedience God still listened to Jonah and gave him another chance.

Ezekiel obeyed God; leading him to have to do some incredibly awkward, humiliating, and 'interesting' things.

Jesus listened to God throughout His life and ministry here on earth, but never so obviously as He did the night He was arrested. Prior to His arrest, Jesus prayed; asking if there was any other way to bring about salvation for you and me. God said no, and Jesus' reply was "Your will be done".

The act of prayer is an act of communication, but it is also what we call a spiritual discipline. The term itself is not found in the Bible, but is one the Church uses to define those things necessary to become more mature and solid in your relationship with God. They are things we need to make part of our character and normal daily lives. You can see by the definition that prayer most certainly falls into that category.

Chapter 2: How to Pray

Jesus out and out told us how we should pray in the Sermon on the Mount (Matthew 5-7). We refer to this instruction in how to pray as the Lord's Prayer. His instruction is primarily what to pray *for* or *about* rather than actually how to pray, so we're going to save that passage of scripture for another chapter. Instead, we're going to look at how to pray as in what our attitude and approach to prayer should be.

Approaching God in Faith

Let's look at a few verses in the Bible on the subject of approaching God in prayer in faith. In doing so we will discover that faith is the key to hearing and receiving God's answers to our prayers.

Therefore I say unto you, What things soever ye desire, when ye pray, believe that ye receive them, and ye shall have them. ~Mark 11:24

This one (and similar verses) are most likely the most misunderstood verse in the Bible. If not, it definitely rates in the top three. Why? Because it is taken out of context, that's why. If you read the verses just prior to this, you will find that Jesus is speaking to the disciples about faith. He tells them that if they have a strong enough faith they can do anything in His name. He then tells them that whatever they ask for they can have, as well. But this is what is called an implied statement. Jesus is implying (not specifically mentioning because the suggestion or understanding is already there) that they wouldn't ask for anything outside the perimeters of one living a faithful, obedient life.

In other words, you wouldn't ask for things that would draw your heart, soul, and mind away from the Father or the Son. You would ask for things (material and otherwise) that would be of physical, emotional, and spiritual benefit to you and to others.

And this is the confidence that we have in him, that, if we ask any thing according to his will, he heareth us: and if we know that he hear us, whatsoever we ask, we know that we have the petitions that we desired of him. `1st John 5:14-15

If ye abide in me, and my words abide in you, ye shall ask what ye will, and it shall be done unto you. ~John 15:7

And all things, whatsoever ye shall ask in prayer, believing, ye shall receive. ~Matthew 21:22

Both of these verses are also on the end of Jesus' comments about the need for faith and being one with Him—heart, soul, and mind.

But let him ask in faith, nothing wavering. For he that wavereth is like a wave of the sea driven with the wind and tossed. For let not that man think that he shall receive any thing of the Lord. A double minded man is unstable in all his ways. ~James 1:6-8

Praying without having faith is like stopping at all the green lights because you don't have faith they will stay green long enough for you to make it through the intersection.

But without faith it is impossible to please him: for he that cometh to God must believe that he is, and that he is a rewarder of them that diligently seek him. ~Hebrews 11:6

This is one of the most beautiful yet telling verses in the Bible. God promises to reward anyone who diligently seeks Him, but reminds us that this is not possible unless we have a faith that is rock-solid. He knows there will be times when we question whether

He is listening because we aren't getting the results we want when we want them. The faith He is talking about here is the faith that never loses sight of the fact that God is real, holy, almighty – and ultimately in control.

Pray Persistently

Pray without ceasing. ~1st Thessalonians 5:17

Call unto me, and I will answer thee, and show thee great and mighty things, which thou knowest not. ~Jeremiah 33:3

Keep asking. Keep talking. Keep listening. God will answer by giving you the promptings of the Holy Spirit, through the works and encouragement of others, and through the events in your life that too many people chalk up to coincidence, happenstance, and fate.

And he spake a parable unto them to this end, that men ought always to pray, and not to faint; Saying, There was in a city a judge, which feared not God, neither regarded man: And there was a widow in that city; and she came unto him, saying, Avenge me of mine adversary. And he would not for a while: but afterward he said within himself, Though I fear not God, nor regard man; yet because this widow troubleth me, I will avenge her, lest by her continual coming she weary me. And the Lord said, Hear what the unjust judge saith. And shall not God avenge his own elect, which cry day and night unto him, though he bear long with them? I tell you that he will avenge them speedily. Nevertheless when the Son of man cometh, shall he find faith on the earth? ~Luke 18:1-18

Jesus' parable is a reminder that God often wants or needs to know how serious or determined we are for what we pray for. Are we genuinely ready for whatever? Are we resolved to handle His answer?

Pray in Agreement with God

Delight thyself also in the Lord: and he shall give thee the desires of thine heart. ~Psalm 37:4

When we are living obediently and faithfully to God, He will give us the desires of our heart because the first desire of our heart will be to do God's will and those that follow will be in line with what God created us to do and be.

Confess your faults one to another, and pray one for another, that ye may be healed. The effectual fervent prayer of a righteous man availeth much. ~James 5:16

For if ye forgive men their trespasses, your heavenly Father will also forgive you: But if ye forgive not men their trespasses, neither will your Father forgive your trespasses. ~Matthew 6:14-15

God cannot and will not answer the prayers of those who refuse to confess their sins to Him or those who refuse to forgive those who have sinned against them.

If my people, which are called by my name, shall humble themselves, and pray, and seek my face, and turn from their wicked ways; then will I hear from heaven, and will forgive their sin, and will heal their land. ~2nd Chronicles 7:14

We must be willing to humble ourselves to the authority and sovereignty of God. We must acknowledge God as the giver of all *because it is all His to give*.

Pray Expecting Answers

My voice shalt thou hear in the morning, O Lord; in the morning will I direct my prayer unto thee, and will look up. ~Psalm 5:3

David looked up because he knew God was going to answer him. He just knew. I love that because it just shows how sure David was of his God. We should be just as sure today.

Be careful for nothing; but in every thing by prayer and supplication with thanksgiving let your requests be made known unto God. And the peace of God, which passeth all understanding, shall keep your hearts and minds through Christ Jesus. ~Philippians 4:6-7

He shall call upon me, and I will answer him: I will be with him in trouble; I will deliver him, and honour him. ~Psalm 91:15

The promise of God should be enough to let us know that our prayers will be answered.

It is important to remember, though, that answered prayer isn't always answered the way we want or think it should be.

No parent always tells their child yes, so why should God be any different? He is the God of the 'big picture'. He knows what is going to be and what is best for us in the days, weeks, and years ahead.

But they that wait upon the Lord shall renew their strength; they shall mount up with wings as eagles; they shall run, and not be weary; and they shall walk, and not faint. ~Isaiah 40:31

God's timing is always the perfect timing. We need to remember this—to not get tired of waiting and to not refuse the strength and comfort He offers while we wait. We must also be mindful of not refusing to see God's answer to our prayer if it differs from what we think it should be.

If not, hearken unto me: hold thy peace, and I shall teach thee wisdom. ~Job 33:33

This verse from Job reminds us that in order for God to answer our prayers we have to be quiet long enough to hear Him. Job wanted answers but was too busy telling God he wanted them to hear God speaking. But God got Job's attention—just like He will get ours.

In faith, with persistence and expectation and a heart that longs to be right with God—this is the 'recipe' for how to pray.

Chapter 3: Why Pray

We know what Prayer is and How to Pray . . . But Why Pray? Answering the Why is to understand the motivation behind your actions let me start out by asking this, why do you talk to your best friend, your spouse, your employer, or other people around you? Now sometimes you may not want to talk to your spouse, your employer or even your best friend because of whatever issues that are between you or maybe because you know you're in trouble with your employer.

The fact remains, however, despite whatever the circumstances are in our daily life between these individuals we have to communicate and interact with them just about every day. Why should it be any different with your relationship with God – the one that created you and gave you life?

The short answer is it should not be any different, well let me back up, it should be different if you truly know who God is. So that's the question, who is God to you? When you answer this question you're going to be one step closer to answering a very personal question, why pray? Now sure there are basic reasons why we should all pray but it really boils down to your relationship with God and who God is to you. The more that you read His Word, the more that you spend time with God in prayer, the more that you draw close to Him the more the God will mean to you.

Recently Valentine's Day had just passed, now I'm not a fan of this particular holiday if that's what you want to call it because I feel that you should be showing your love each and every day to the person that you're with. Nevertheless it brings me to a point to help you better understand something here.

For those that are married do you remember falling in love with your spouse? Do you remember what it was like to have that all-consuming desire and love for them? Do you remember how you couldn't wait until you were able to see them again or talk with them again? We need to have a love relationship with Jesus Christ in a similar fashion. Now I am not talking about a romantic love but a passionate love nonetheless that seeks to have a servant's heart and a sincere desire to do God's will.

Interesting enough if we look at couples that have been married for a long period of time often times you will find the spark has died, they may barely see each other because of work, and hardly ever speak except for talking about the necessities of life such as bills and the kids. This is a great example of how most of our prayer lives are with God.

We have to get back that spark – do you remember when you first came to the Lord how passionate and on fire you were to serve Him and to pray and communicate with him?

Brothers and sisters it's time for a revival within each of us and then collectively as we organically come together in the spirit – let's start a resurrection and a revival once again, and let it start right now within each of us. And then you will understand why you need to pray.

Continuing on with the relationship theme, how many marriages end in divorce because of adultery, abuse or neglect? How many of us have a prayer life that is in similar disarray?

If you’re not praying to God but you’re sitting in front of the television for hours each day or listening to music is this not adultery if you do not make equal time for God? Are you abusing your relationship with God by only coming to Him in prayer when you need or want something? Are you neglecting your relationship with Almighty God potentially because of sin that is crêpe in and now hold you captive?

Let me explain how the pattern works brothers and sisters first it starts with neglect then it leads to abuse and ultimately adultery or idolatry as the Bible describes it. It’s a vicious cycle but one that can be broken with the blood of the lamb, one that can be broken through committing yourself to learning and getting close to God both in His Word and in Prayer.

Why Pray? Well here's some basic answers:

- Because You Love God
- To Keep Your Relationship with God Strong
- Because You love your family, friends, country etc
- Because you want to see God's will done on Earth as it is in heaven
- To Fight Back Against your Spiritual Enemy
- To Walk in the Authority God has Given You

Remember, prayer is a tangible real thing that should not be discarded or put to the side until you have an emergency or crisis. Is that the kind of relationship you want someone to have with you? Learn to have a good relationship with God by talking with Him daily in prayer.

So many of us continue to struggle and have such a poor prayer life because we don't recognize prayer for what it truly is and just how powerful it is. It should not be your last resort – it should be your immediate response to situations, circumstances, and dealing with our spiritual enemy's attacks.

You must learn to see these attacks for what they are and address them accordingly in prayer – taking authority over the enemy in the name of Jesus. How many of us understand and recognize that every single day of our lives we are in a spiritual war and that prayer is essential for living a victorious life in Christ? Now is the time to Pray!

Chapter 4:

Making Time to Pray

Making time to pray is one of the biggest complaints and hurdles Christians say they are faced with. I get it—life is hectic. We have all sorts of people and things vying for our time and attention. It only seems practical or reasonable to put the things that are staring us in the face first. But oh, what a mistake that is!

To help put it into perspective, let me ask you the following questions:

- Would you consider eating dinner and going to bed instead of picking your child up from sports practice or piano lessons because you are at home and able to *see* dinner cooking on the stove and your bedroom, but cannot see your child while they are at practice/lessons?

- Would you consider not paying your insurance premiums in order to buy new furniture because you can see the furniture but not the benefits of having the insurance?
- Would you not call your parents or grandparents to talk with them or check on their well-being if seeing them on a regular basis was not possible? You know, the 'out of sight, out of mind' philosophy?

I am hoping and praying you answered each of these questions with an emphatic NO. Why, then, do you relegate God and prayer to a status of 'bottom of the totem pole' (last place)?

Whether or not you make time to pray shouldn't be the question. The question should be what you have time for *after* you pray. You might have to give up a television show, a few less minutes in the book you are reading, one less round of golf, or take one less class at the gym, but prayer should take precedence over the activities in your life.

How to make time to pray

If your response to the last statement is something resembling denial that you are too busy or that you cannot possibly give up *that,* you seriously need to re-think your priorities. That being said, I don't want you to feel that what you do with your day is of no importance or significance. That is why I want to offer you the following suggestions on how to make time to pray:

- Set aside a special time for prayer each day. A time of completely being focused on conversing with God is essential in your relationship with Him. Think about it: you wouldn't appreciate it if your spouse or your children never took the time to focus on talking to you. You would feel slighted and unimportant. You would feel you were in the way and an inconvenient duty rather than a treasured and cherished loved one.

This is exactly how God feels when we fit Him in when we have a minute here and there or if we are in over our heads and need His divine intervention. By taking the time to be solely focused on prayer each day, you will know God so much more intimately; making it possible for you to avoid many of the issues people use to distance themselves from seeking God's face each day.

- Pray before all Meals and as a Family
- Pray before you drive anywhere and Pray as you are driving: hands on the wheel, eyes on the road, pray for safety, pray for those you meet on the road, pray for the ability to be a witness of God's goodness in all you do and say throughout your day.

- Pray while fixing your kids' breakfast or lunch. Pray for their safety, that they will make right choices, and that they will seek to have a personal relationship with God each and every day of their lives.
- Pray while taking a walk. Pray for your community, your church, our government and military, and for those you know who have specific needs.
- Pray when you first open your eyes each morning. Thank God for the rest you enjoyed, for His amazing grace, for the fact that He is God, and for the precious gift of salvation.
- Pray when you lay your head on the pillow at night. When you make conversation and thoughts of God among the last ones you have each night, you can go to sleep with the peace that passes all understanding.

FYI: Often time's people say they feel guilty falling asleep at night in the middle of their prayers. But I will share with you something I read a while back on that very subject: nothing could be sweeter than drifting off to sleep while talking with your creator. What better company could you possibly have?

Again, I know it isn't always easy to push the hustle and bustle of life out of the way, but for anyone who claims Jesus as Savior, it is something you simply must do in order to make your words more than just lip service. Making prayer a priority is also worth it - Always worth it.

To give you a bit of encouragement and inspiration take a few minutes to read through the following Bible verses. I also encourage and challenge you to commit at least two or three of them to memory so that they can serve as your reminders each and every day.

Pray without ceasing. ~1st Thessalonians 5:17

Any time is a good time to pray. Prayer can be a few words spoken out loud or mentally spoken. Prayer can be a cry for help, a shout of praise, a desperate plea, or a heart to heart conversation that lasts as long as it needs to last.

Likewise the Spirit also helpeth our infirmities: for we know not what we should pray for as we ought: but the Spirit itself maketh intercession for us with groanings which cannot be uttered. ~Romans 8:26

I know someone whose prayer is simply this: "LORD, I know You know what is best and that all things work out for Your good, so please just give me the faith, courage, and strength to hold on for the ride."

But thou, when thou prayest, enter into thy closet, and when thou hast shut thy door, pray to thy Father which is in secret; and thy Father which seeth in secret shall reward thee openly. ~Matthew 6:6

This is the time we spend in focused, personal prayer.

What is it then? I will pray with the spirit, and I will pray with the understanding also: I will sing with the spirit, and I will sing with the understanding also. ~1st Corinthians 14:15

Prayers can also be songs, short and simple words of praise, and thank-yous for God's protection, comfort, and active presence in situations.

Praying always with all prayer and supplication in the Spirit, and watching thereunto with all perseverance and supplication for all saints ~Ephesians 6:18

As for me, I will call upon God; and the Lord shall save me. Evening, and morning, and at noon, will I pray, and cry aloud: and he shall hear my voice. ~Psalm 55:16-17

Again…there's never a bad time to pray.

Chapter 5:

Praying the Scriptures

What does it mean to 'pray the scriptures'? The best way to explain it is to pray God's will to be done. It sounds simple because it is. It is also something I can show you better than I can tell you.

Praying the scriptures

Praying for a spouse: *And the Lord God said, It is not good that the man should be alone; I will make him an help meet for him. ~Genesis 2:18*

Praying to know God's will for your life: *For I know the thoughts that I think toward you, saith the Lord, thoughts of peace, and not of evil, to give you an expected end. ~Jeremiah 29:11*

Praying to be more God-centered and a kingdom worker: *But seek ye first the kingdom of God, and his righteousness; and all these things shall be added unto you. ~Matthew 6:33*

Prayer of thanks for your wife: *Whoso findeth a wife findeth a good thing, and obtaineth favour of the LORD. ~Proverbs 18:22*

Pray for increased faith to see God's answers to your prayers: *And blessed is she that believed: for there shall be a performance of those things which were told her from the Lord. ~Luke 1:45*

Pray for Godly parenting skills: *And blessed is she that believed: for there shall be a performance of those things which were told her from the Lord. ~Ephesians 6:4*

Pray for a Godly marriage*: Wives, submit yourselves unto your own husbands, as unto the Lord. Husbands, love your wives, even as Christ also loved the church, and gave himself for it; ~Ephesians 5:22 and 25*

Prayers of thanks for God's gift of salvation: *But God commendeth his love toward us, in that, while we were yet sinners, Christ died for us. ~Romans 5:8*

Pray for the ability to treat those who hurt and persecute you: *But I say unto you, Love your enemies, bless them that curse you, do good to them that hate you, and pray for them which despitefully use you, and persecute you. ~Matthew 5:44*

Prayer of thanks for your friends and loved ones: *I thank my God always on your behalf, for the grace of God which is given you by Jesus Christ ~1st Corinthians 1:4*

Pray for the Church to grow: *Pray ye therefore the Lord of the harvest, that he will send forth labourers into his harvest. ~Matthew 9:38*

Pray to know the mind of Christ for your life: *Ye ask, and receive not, because ye ask amiss, that ye may consume it upon your lusts. ~James 4:3*

Pray for your government and the leaders you work and live under: *I exhort therefore, that, first of all, supplications, prayers, intercessions, and giving of thanks, be made for all men; For kings, and for all that are in authority; that we may lead a quiet and peaceable life in all godliness and honesty. For this is good and acceptable in the sight of God our Saviour; Who will have all men to be saved, and to come unto the knowledge of the truth. ~1st Timothy 2:1-4*

Pray for the lost: *Brethren, my heart's desire and prayer to God for Israel is, that they might be saved. ~Romans 10:1*

Hopefully seeing the scriptures paired with the prayer you can pray helps in understanding what it means to 'pray the scripture'. But just in case it doesn't, here are some examples of what it 'looks like'…

Father, thank You for loving me. Thank You for salvation and your unconditional love. Father, I ask that you give me a heart that seeks Your kingdom and Your righteousness in my life. I pray You will be my first priority in all things because I know when I live my life in this way You will supply all my needs. (Matthew 6:33) In Jesus' name I pray, amen.

Or...

Father, God, You have said that it is not good for man to be alone. That is why I come to you asking for You to send me the someone I can spend my life with. Send me that special someone who I will love and cherish all the days of my life. I pray he/she will be gentle, faithful to You and to me, and that we can work together to raise children who call You LORD. In Jesus' name I pray, amen. (Genesis 2:18)

Why pray the scriptures

Praying the scriptures serves several purposes—all of which are good and serve to help you grow spiritually. Praying the scriptures:

- Keeps you in focus to pray God's will for yourself and for others
- Makes you more knowledgeable of the Word
- Allows you to 'cover all the bases' of prayer (thanksgiving, confession, praise, intercession, petition)
- Gives you a more God-centered attitude about life in general

How to pray the scriptures

Praying the scriptures is often done while reading the Bible or during those times when your prayers are brief conversations with specific concerns and/or observations are being made. For example…

If you were reading the book of Proverbs in your daily Bible reading/study, you might pray, "LORD, let me cry out for wisdom and knowledge as the writer of Proverbs tells me to so that I will understand what it means to fear and respect You." (Proverbs 2:3 & 5)

Or…

When you are moved by the words of the preacher in a worship service, you might pray, "I am not ashamed of the Gospel and I want You to know, God, that I am committed to living and speaking its truth each and every day with bold grace." (Romans 1:16)

Praying the scriptures won't constitute your entire prayer life, but it will definitely enhance its quality and depth.

Chapter 6:

Praying for God's Will to be Done

Similar to praying the Scriptures in the previous chapter, praying for God's will be done is closely related. When you are praying the Scriptures you are praying for specific things that may or may not relate directly to you. God may have specific plans just for you and unfortunately many of us don't know or understand what our calling truly is.

While praying for a wife, wisdom, or the ability to love your enemies are all great things to pray for – what if God's desire for you is not to be married or have children, will you still love Him?

See we don't always get what we want and not everything in Scripture applies directly to us personally -attempting to apply such a philosophy to Scripture would be an error. It's at these crucial times that we literally Pray for God's will to be done on earth as it is in heaven in our lives – in every aspect of our lives. Pray and ask God to open the doors that He would have you walk through and closed the doors tightly that He would not have you walk through.

Remember Praying without believing is like faith without works – one has to accompany the other to be complete and true. Also remember to keep it real with God, do not simply just pay Him lip service – you're literally wasting your breath.

If you're going to pray for God's will to be done on earth as it is in heaven in your life you have to be ready to accept what that means and what comes next. I think many of us lack the necessary courage and faith to walk out God's will for our lives. Praying for the necessary courage and faith to walk it out would no doubt be a great prayer if you find yourself doubting or fearful – pray against those things immediately and take authority over them in Jesus name.

Chapter 7:

Jesus Example of Prayer

Jesus Example of Prayer in John 17:

These words spake Jesus, and lifted up his
eyes to heaven, and said, Father, the hour is
come; glorify thy Son, that thy Son also may
glorify thee: [2]As thou hast given him power
over all flesh, that he should give eternal life
to as many as thou hast given him. [3]And this
is life eternal, that they might know thee the
only true God, and Jesus Christ, whom thou
hast sent. [4] I have glorified thee on the earth:
I have finished the work which thou gavest
me to do. [5]And now, O Father, glorify thou
me with thine own self with the glory which
I had with thee before the world was. [6] I
have manifested thy name unto the men
which thou gavest me out of the world: thine
they were, and thou gavest them me; and
they have kept thy word. [7] Now they have
known that all things whatsoever thou hast
given me are of thee.

[8] For I have given unto them the words
which thou gavest me; and they have
received them, and have known surely that I
came out from thee, and they have believed
that thou didst send me. [9] I pray for them: **I
pray not for the world**, but for them which
thou hast given me; for they are thine. [10]
And all mine are thine, and thine are mine;
and I am glorified in them. [11] And now I am
no more in the world, but these are in the
world, and I come to thee. Holy Father, keep
through thine own name those whom thou
hast given me, that they may be one, as we
are. [12] While I was with them in the world, I
kept them in thy name: those that thou
gavest me I have kept, and none of them is
lost, but the son of perdition; that the
scripture might be fulfilled. [13] And now
come I to thee; and these things I speak in
the world, that they might have my joy
fulfilled in themselves. [14] I have given them
thy word; and the world hath hated them,
because they are not of the world, even as I
am not of the world. [15] I pray not that thou
shouldest take them out of the world, **but
that thou shouldest keep them from the
evil**.

[16] They are not of the world, even as I am
not of the world. [17] **Sanctify them through
thy truth: thy word is truth.** [18] As thou
hast sent me into the world, even so have I
also sent them into the world. [19] And for
their sakes I sanctify myself, that they also
might be sanctified through the truth. **[20]**
**Neither pray I for these alone, but for
them also which shall believe on me
through their word;** [21] That they all may be
one; as thou, Father, art in me, and I in thee,
that they also may be one in us: that the
world may believe that thou hast sent me. [22]
And the glory which thou gavest me I have
given them; that they may be one, even as
we are one: [23] I in them, and thou in me, that
they may be made perfect in one; and that
the world may know that thou hast sent me,
and hast loved them, as thou hast loved me.
[24] Father, I will that they also, whom thou
hast given me, be with me where I am; that
they may behold my glory, which thou hast
given me: for thou lovedst me before the
foundation of the world. [25] O righteous

Father, the world hath not known thee: but I have known thee, and these have known that thou hast sent me. 26 And I have declared unto them thy name, and will declare it: that the love wherewith thou hast loved me may be in them, and I in them.

This may in fact be Jesus's longest prayer that is recorded in the New Testament, let's look at some key things that stand out in this prayer. First and foremost it's important to recognize that in this particular prayer Jesus does not pray for the world but for those that believe in Him – His disciples and those that would believe because of the disciple's words. Jesus also prays that his father would keep them from evil and sanctify them through God's word. It's amazing that over 2000 years ago when Christ prayed these words that He was thinking about you and I who believe in Him because of the apostles words written down in the Holy Bible. What an awesome God we serve.

In this prayer we read how Jesus interacts with the father – does your prayer life look like this? How do you pray for the disciples that you should be making? How do you pray for future generations that will believe because of those disciples' words? Are you even making disciples? Are you going about your father's business – will you hear the words well done good and faithful servant? In this prayer Jesus knows He is about to return back to the father and that His time is short, it's almost like He's reviewing a checklist for things that he needed to do while He was on earth.

We, however, do not know when our time on this earth will be completed therefore it is critical to pray with a sense of urgency as if eternity is just around the corner. The more that you study this specific prayer the more you will have insight into the heart of Jesus Christ.

"The Lord's Prayer"

Jesus' words to His disciples in regards to instructing them (and us) how to pray are what we refer to as the Lord's Prayer. The passage of scripture found in Matthew 6 is often recited and memorized as an actual prayer. Quite honestly, however, this is not what it was intended to be. Jesus' intentions weren't for us to recite His words. His intentions were for us to pattern our prayers according to His outline'.

This might bring up the question of whether or not it is wrong to pray the Lord's Prayer. My answer to that would be no—that it is not *wrong*, but I would add to that by saying it is not really beneficial to do so. I say this because:

- The Lord's Prayer is not *personal* and from the heart—as prayer should be.
- Praying the Lord's Prayer might be considered praying the scripture, but unless you make it specific, you are reciting, not praying.

That being said…the Lord's Prayer is a good way to teach yourself or others how to stay focused on praying for and about the things we need to pray for. So let's take a look at the Lord's Prayer; taking it apart line by line to see what Jesus is wanting us to learn from His model prayer.

After this manner therefore pray ye: Our Father which art in heaven, Hallowed be thy name. Thy kingdom come, Thy will be done in earth, as it is in heaven. Give us this day our daily bread. And forgive us our debts, as we forgive our debtors. And lead us not into temptation, but deliver us from evil: For thine is the kingdom, and the power, and the glory, forever. Amen. ~Matthew 6:9-13

Our Father in heaven, hallowed be thy name: Recognizing God for who He is should always be first in your daily prayer sessions. When you recognize God you are naturally humbled. Doing so also prepares your heart for speaking, listening, and obeying because it affirms your faith and belief in God's holiness.

God isn't picky when it comes to what you say to 'hallow His name'. A simple thank-you for being God will do, but it isn't difficult to come up with a whole lot more than that. You can also praise God for His holiness by recognizing any of the many attributes of His character. For example, some of the character traits the Bible attributes to God include:

- Personally interested—God is personally interested in every little detail of your life. He has the hairs on your head numbered as well as the days of your life. He has a lot invested in you and is constantly watching and waiting for a return on that investment.
- Creator of all—all of creation is God's to do with as He pleases. To praise God for the intricate workings of nature should be as natural as breathing.

- Vine pruner—God prunes and shapes our lives so that we can live out our purpose. Discipline is a part of growing and maturing. To expect otherwise is prideful and honestly, quite delusional. Who are we to think God shouldn't correct us? When done correctly, discipline is an excellent teacher as well as serving to hone our skills and character. FYI: God always 'does discipline' the right way.
- Truth—God's Word is true and unchanging and He is always good for the many promises He has made.
- Savior—God's mercy and unconditional love are the only reason we have salvation from sin that offers the opportunity to spend eternity with Him.
- Eternal—God is forever and nothing is going to change that.
- Forgiving—when we sincerely ask forgiveness God is always ready, willing, and able to forgive. This is the greatest attribute of all.

Thy kingdom come, Thy will be done in earth, as it is in heaven. I am quite certain that most people reciting these words don't truly understand what it is they are saying or asking for. I am also equally certain they don't realize the responsibility they are signing on for when they say these words. I don't say this to be critical or to sound as if I am on a higher level of spirituality. I am simply trying to help each of us come to a more intimate and genuine level of communication with God. So let's take a closer look at this phrase and what it really means…

Thy kingdom come. Jesus is really saying two things here.

1) He is saying we should be praying with anticipation for God to sound the trumpet for the second coming of Christ. That's pretty straightforward and easy to understand. But it is also something many people *say* they look forward to, but…

To ask God to come soon should come from a heart that truly looks forward with assurance and hope for eternity in heaven.

2) Jesus is also talking about the growth of the Kingdom of God here on earth. In many of Jesus' parables He says "..the kingdom of God…" or "…the kingdom of heaven...". In both instances Jesus is referring to you and me here as in the body of saved believers. He is instructing us to pray for the development of the Kingdom of God within us and for the Kingdom to grow and spread across the world so that as many as possible might come to know Jesus as Savior. This is definitely something we should be praying for.

Now for our role in this: in praying for the growth and spreading of the Kingdom of God, we are saying we will do our part to make that happen.

We are basically saying, "Bring on the Great Commission! I'm ready to get down to the business of making Disciples!"

But are you? Am I? Are we really willing to help God's kingdom increase here on earth? If so, what are we actively doing to try to make that happen in our own little corner of the world?

Thy will be done in earth, as it is in heaven. This is simply Jesus' way of emphasizing what He had just said—to remind us that God's kingdom wasn't just some far-off place. Jesus was reminding us that we have a job to do here on earth and that job is to be God's living, breathing, and active representatives of His Kingdom. We are to be about the business of God each and every day of our lives. This sentence in the model prayer is to remind us that we shouldn't be shy or scared to ask God for a daily supply of courage, strength, wisdom, compassion, discernment, and love to be who and what we are supposed to be.

Give us this day our daily bread. We are to ask God for the things we need—bread and everything else.

Sometimes we are so naïve. Or maybe it's pride. Either way we are often blind to the fact that everything we have belongs to God. He gives us the ability to earn a salary from which we buy the things we enjoy and have to have, but it all goes back to the fact that *He gives us the ability.*

Asking God to provide our needs and the desires of our heart humbles us to recognize our inability to make due on our own and the fact that these things are God's to give as He pleases. We are expressing our need for God's care and provision.

And forgive us our debts, as we forgive our debtors. The words 'debt' and 'debtors' in the original Greek means 'that which is due'. Using this direct translation of the word, let's look at what Jesus is saying:

Forgive us for not giving You that which is due in the same way we forgive those who don't give us that which is due us.

I see a bit of Jesus' irony coming out here. He is instructing us to ask God for the same measure of forgiveness we extend to others. Ouch!

By instructing us in this way, Jesus is reminding us of three things:

1) Jesus is reminding us of our need for grace—that none of us is any more deserving of God's favor than the person next to us.
2) Jesus is reminding us that we are all sinners and that in God's eyes no sin is greater than another.
3) Jesus is reminding us of what He had just said about loving our enemies, not holding grudges, and going the extra mile (Matthew 5).

Immediately following the model for prayer, Jesus goes on to say this:

For if ye forgive men their trespasses, your heavenly Father will also forgive you: But if ye forgive not men their trespasses, neither will your Father forgive your trespasses. ~Matthew 6:14-15

The word 'trespasses' in the Greek is translated 'to step over' or 'sin'. I'm not sure why He used the word 'trespass' here and the word 'debtor' in giving us the model prayer, but it is obvious He is tying the two together. He knows that an unforgiving heart cannot be in alignment with doing the will of God. That is why He instructed us to pray this for ourselves each and every day.

And lead us not into temptation, but deliver us from evil… When I read this I think of the old hymn, "I Need Thee Every Hour". Part of it goes like this:

I need Thee every hour; stay close and nearby. Temptations lose their power when You are close by. I need Thee, Oh, I need Thee. Every hour I need Thee. Oh, bless me now my Savior, I come to Thee.

The Bible tells us in no uncertain terms that neither God nor Jesus tempts us—that temptation comes from the devil. He plants it like seeds in our hearts and minds. He puts it before us in cunning disguises, but it is always from him. The devil is also very persuasive in his ability to tempt us. Jesus knows that. He also knows that we need to stay in prayer if we are going to walk in victory against the devil and his minions.

For thine is the kingdom, and the power, and the glory, forever. Amen. The ending of our prayer should be to bring it full-circle; putting the focus back on God. Ending our prayer time by giving God the glory and recognition he deserves is only fitting. Ending our prayers this way also serves as just one more reminder of the fact that we are reliant on and hopeful in God.

There are a number of things people do to assist them in establishing a consistent prayer life. We're going to look at several of them in the next chapter, but I want to close this section of the book by saying that when it comes to the 'mechanics' of prayer, Jesus' model prayer is much more than an idea or suggestion. It is an instruction…command, even…from Jesus the Savior and only Son of God.

Chapter 8:

Learning to be a Prayer Warrior

A prayer warrior—sounds a little intimidating, doesn't it? Don't worry, though. It's not. A prayer warrior is merely a term used to describe someone who is vigilant and ceaseless in their prayers. A prayer warrior is someone who knows and counts on the power of prayer to bring about change and blessing in their life and the lives of others. A Prayer Warrior is someone who understands there is a Spiritual War going on all the time. They intercede for themselves and others by binding, rebuking, and taking authority over the enemy through faith and prayer. A prayer warrior is someone who understands the power of prayer and the authority Christ has given us and operates in faith and courage to do battle against spiritual forces of darkness.

I mentioned at the conclusion of a previous chapter that there are several methods people use to help them establish a strong and consistent prayer life. We're going to look at a few of them now in an effort to help you do the same.

Pray without ceasing

You have seen this verse sprinkled throughout the pages of this book and here it is again: *Pray without ceasing. ~1st Thessalonians 5:17* Your mom always told you that practice makes perfect when it came time to practice your music lessons, or learn your multiplication facts. Well, the same holds true for the discipline of prayer. Practice makes perfect. The more you pray the more you will want to pray and the more you want to pray the more reliant you will become on God. And that, my friend, is about as perfect as it gets this side of heaven.

ACTS Acronym

Adoration: Giving God the glory, praise and honor due Him. Praising God for creation and for His forever-ness.

- *Who being the brightness of his glory, and the express image of his person, and upholding all things by the word of his power, when he had by himself purged our sins, sat down on the right hand of the Majesty on high: ~Hebrews 1:3*
- *And every creature which is in heaven, and on the earth, and under the earth, and such as are in the sea, and all that are in them, heard I saying, Blessing, and honour, and glory, and power, be unto him that sitteth upon the throne, and unto the Lamb for ever and ever. ~Revelation 5:13*
- *And thou shalt love the Lord thy God with all thy heart, and with all thy soul, and with all thy mind, and with all thy strength: this is the first commandment. ~Mark 12:30*

- *Praise ye the Lord. Praise God in his sanctuary: praise him in the firmament of his power. Praise him for his mighty acts: praise him according to his excellent greatness. Praise him with the sound of the trumpet: praise him with the psaltery and harp. Praise him with the timbrel and dance: praise him with stringed instruments and organs. Praise him upon the loud cymbals: praise him upon the high sounding cymbals. Let every thing that hath breath praise the Lord. Praise ye the Lord. ~Psalm 150*

Confession: Confessing your sins to God specifically, humbly, and with a heart of true repentance.

- *If we confess our sins, he is faithful and just to forgive us our sins, and to cleanse us from all unrighteousness. ~1st John 1:9*
- *He that covereth his sins shall not prosper: but whoso confesseth and forsaketh them shall have mercy. ~Proverbs 28:13*

- *Submit yourselves therefore to God. Resist the devil, and he will flee from you. Draw nigh to God, and he will draw nigh to you. Cleanse your hands, ye sinners; and purify your hearts, ye double minded. Be afflicted, and mourn, and weep: let your laughter be turned to mourning, and your joy to heaviness. Humble yourselves in the sight of the Lord, and he shall lift you up. ~James 4:7-10*
- *Have mercy upon me, O God, according to thy lovingkindness: according unto the multitude of thy tender mercies blot out my transgressions. Wash me throughly from mine iniquity, and cleanse me from my sin. For I acknowledge my transgressions: and my sin is ever before me. ~Psalm 51:1-3*

Thanksgiving: Give thanks to God for His blessings, His love, His mercy, His gift of salvation, and for the hope of heaven.

- *Giving thanks always for all things unto God and the Father in the name of our Lord Jesus Christ; ~Ephesians 5:20*
- *O give thanks unto the God of heaven: for his mercy endureth for ever. ~Psalm 136:26*
- *Bless the Lord, O my soul, and forget not all his benefits... ~Psalm 103:2*
- *Enter into his gates with thanksgiving, and into his courts with praise: be thankful unto him, and bless his name. ~Psalm 100:4*

Supplication: Praying on behalf of others and asking for the things we need and desire is definitely a part of prayer. Remember: prayer is communicating with God for the purpose of developing a deeper relationship with Him. That cannot happen if we aren't honest with God and if we don't open ourselves up completely to Him.

- *And this is the confidence that we have in him, that, if we ask any thing according to his will, he heareth us... ~1st John 5:14*
- *Ye ask, and receive not, because ye ask amiss, that ye may consume it upon your lusts. ~James 4:3*
- *But let him ask in faith, nothing wavering. For he that wavereth is like a wave of the sea driven with the wind and tossed. For let not that man think that he shall receive any thing of the Lord. A double minded man is unstable in all his ways. ~James 1:6-8*
- *My help cometh from the Lord, which made heaven and earth. ~Psalm 121:2*
- *Come unto me, all ye that labour and are heavy laden, and I will give you rest. ~Matthew 11:28*
- *And the Lord turned the captivity of Job, when he prayed for his friends: also the Lord gave Job twice as much as he had before. ~Job 42:10*

PRAY Acronym

The PRAY acronym is another often-used method of developing good prayer habits. As you can see, it is quite similar to the ACTS acronym, but then why wouldn't it be? They all follow the model prayer (the LORD's prayer) in Matthew 6.

There is, however, one aspect of the PRAY acronym I think needs to be highlighted. It is the Y, which reminds us to yield to God's purpose for our lives. So while I won't take the time to repeat every scripture used above for the ACTS acronym, I will insert a few of them in the appropriate place then focus on some that deal with yielding to God's will.

Praise: Giving God the glory, praise and honor due Him. Praising God for creation and for His forever-ness.

- *Who being the brightness of his glory, and the express image of his person, and upholding all things by the word of his power, when he had by himself purged our sins, sat down on the right hand of the Majesty on high: ~Hebrews 1:3*
- *And every creature which is in heaven, and on the earth, and under the earth, and such as are in the sea, and all that are in them, heard I saying, Blessing, and honour, and glory, and power, be unto him that sitteth upon the throne, and unto the Lamb for ever and ever. ~Revelation 5:13*

Repent: To repent means to change your ways. It is a reversing of yourself from living a sinful lifestyle to a Godly lifestyle.

- *And the times of this ignorance God winked at; but now commandeth all men every where to repent... Acts 17:30*

- *Know ye not that the unrighteous shall not inherit the kingdom of God? Be not deceived: neither fornicators, nor idolaters, nor adulterers, nor effeminate, nor abusers of themselves with mankind, nor thieves, nor covetous, nor drunkards, nor revilers, nor extortioners, shall inherit the kingdom of God. ~1st Corinthians 6:9-10*
- *Then Peter said unto them, Repent, and be baptized every one of you in the name of Jesus Christ for the remission of sins, and ye shall receive the gift of the Holy Ghost. ~Acts 2:38*
- *And be not conformed to this world: but be ye transformed by the renewing of your mind, that ye may prove what is that good, and acceptable, and perfect, will of God. ~Romans 12:2*

- *And fear not them which kill the body, but are not able to kill the soul: but rather fear him which is able to destroy both soul and body in hell. ~Matthew 10:28*

Ask: Asking God for the desires of your heart, for the needs you have in your life, and for the provision and safety for others all comes under this 'category'.

- *Ye ask, and receive not, because ye ask amiss, that ye may consume it upon your lusts. ~James 4:3*
- *But let him ask in faith, nothing wavering. For he that wavereth is like a wave of the sea driven with the wind and tossed. For let not that man think that he shall receive any thing of the Lord. A double minded man is unstable in all his ways. ~James 1:6-8*
- *My help cometh from the Lord, which made heaven and earth. ~Psalm 121:2*

- *Come unto me, all ye that labour and are heavy laden, and I will give you rest. ~Matthew 11:28*

Yield: To yield is to give in—to allow God to have His way in your life. Yielding is submission and obedience. Yielding is also living by faith.

- *For God so loved the world, that he gave his only begotten Son, that whosoever believeth in him should not perish, but have everlasting life. ~John 3:16*
- *What? know ye not that your body is the temple of the Holy Ghost which is in you, which ye have of God, and ye are not your own? ~1st Corinthians 6:19*
- *Trust in the Lord with all thine heart; and lean not unto thine own understanding. In all thy ways acknowledge him, and he shall direct thy paths. Be not wise in thine own eyes: fear the Lord, and depart from evil. ~Proverbs 3:5-7*

- *But be ye doers of the word, and not hearers only, deceiving your own selves. For if any be a hearer of the word, and not a doer, he is like unto a man beholding his natural face in a glass: For he beholdeth himself, and goeth his way, and straightway forgetteth what manner of man he was. But whoso looketh into the perfect law of liberty, and continueth therein, he being not a forgetful hearer, but a doer of the work, this man shall be blessed in his deed. ~James 1:22-25*
- *Be ye therefore followers of God, as dear children. ~Ephesians 5:1*
- *For if we sin wilfully after that we have received the knowledge of the truth, there remaineth no more sacrifice for sins, But a certain fearful looking for of judgment and fiery indignation, which shall devour the adversaries. ~Hebrews 10:26-27*
- *God is a Spirit: and they that worship him must worship him in spirit and in truth. ~John 4:24*

I'll say it again: a prayer warrior is someone who understands, believes in, and depends on the power of prayer. Be a prayer warrior!

Chapter 9:

Praying for Healing

Praying for the healing of self and others is something many of us have difficulty in wrapping our heads and hearts around. We pray believing God will hear us. We pray believing God will give us what we ask for because that is what scripture tells us. We pray, yet much of the time our prayers are not answered in the way we think they should be. Our loved one dies. An innocent child is taken from the loving arms of their parents. Soldiers don't come home.

So what's the matter? Are we praying wrong? Is the Bible lying?

The answers to those questions are as follows:

We may or may not be praying ‘wrong’. While it is never wrong to ask God to heal someone so that we can continue to enjoy loving them here on earth or so that their families can remain intact, our first prayer should always be for God’s will to be done because His will is always perfect and right. Secondly we can pray for those we wish to pray for, but along with those prayers we should ask God for the strength and wisdom necessary to accept His answer.

Right now a young family in the Midwest is praying earnestly for their infant son. He has a somewhat rare disease that has robbed him of his ability to swallow on his own, to sit or stand, and of the ability for his lungs to expel fluid. This little guy has to spend most of his time hooked to one machine or another. He will likely not reach his second birthday. His parents, grandparents, and countless friends, family, and other prayer warriors are praying for baby Logan and his family.

They are praying for miraculous healing. But they are also praying for strength, courage, and wisdom to give him the best of their love for whatever time God gives them together.

No, the Bible is not lying. The Bible tells us that whatever we ask for in God's will it will be done. Yet we have to remember God's will first - Always first.

Keeping that in mind, let's take a look at some of the scriptures dealing with prayers for healing. As you read them, think about how you can be more in tune to God's will and prayers for His children.

Most of all remember this: Healing in its best and truest form is to be with God the Father for all eternity. Not to sound morbid or anything but for those who are saved but dealing with terminal illness, healing is often physical death.

- *Is any among you afflicted? let him pray. Is any merry? let him sing psalms. Is any sick among you? let him call for the elders of the church; and let them pray over him, anointing him with oil in the name of the Lord: And the prayer of faith shall save the sick, and the Lord shall raise him up; and if he have committed sins, they shall be forgiven him. Confess your faults one to another, and pray one for another, that ye may be healed. The effectual fervent prayer of a righteous man availeth much. ~James 5:13-16*
- *And we know that all things work together for good to them that love God, to them who are the called according to his purpose. ~Romans 8:28*

- *Beloved, I wish above all things that thou mayest prosper and be in health, even as thy soul prospereth. ~3rd John 1:2*
- *Who his own self bare our sins in his own body on the tree, that we, being dead to sins, should live unto righteousness: by whose stripes ye were healed. ~1st Peter 2:24*

As I mentioned before when are prayers don't get answered, especially prayers for love ones healing it can cause confusion and doubt in your faith and sometimes even in God. Yet this is a snare of the devil to keep you locked in bondage – learn to break free from the oppression of the devil by walking in faith, encourage, and in the word of God. One way to break free from this oppression in bondage is to develop a checklist of sorts.

Consider the following is a short checklist:

- Is there sin in my life preventing my prayers from being answered
- Do I know for certain what I'm praying is God's will? – If not then pray that God's will would be done on earth as it is in heaven in the situation.
- I'm I being targeted by workers of darkness such as witches, Satanist, and others who practice the dark arts?
- Have I cleansed myself from all generational curses or familiar spirits?
- Is my relationship with God where it needs to be?
- Have I prayed over my house or place of continual prayer?
- Is there an open door that I or my family members have inadvertently opened to enable the spiritual forces of darkness to hinder my prayer life?
- Are there things in my home that are spiritually charged that are affecting my prayer life?
- Have I done my due diligence, and through the Spirit of God attempted to research and rightly divide the Word of God as it pertains to the specific situation?

These are just a few questions to ask yourself when you're prayers are not being answered. Sometimes it's also critical to fast and pray – remember it's a real war and it's here every day.

Chapter 10:

Praying as a Means of Spiritual Warfare

Spiritual Warfare sounds even scarier and more intimidating than the term 'Prayer Warrior'. That's because it can actually be a very scary thing if you don't know what you're doing or who you are in Christ Jesus. Learn from the clear example below in the Word of God not to try this unless you know who you are in Christ.

Acts 19:11-17

*11 Now God worked unusual miracles by
the hands of Paul, 12 so that even
handkerchiefs or aprons were brought
from his body to the sick, and the diseases
left them and the evil spirits went out of
them. 13 Then some of the itinerant Jewish
exorcists took it upon themselves to call the
name of the Lord Jesus over those who had
evil spirits, saying, "We exorcise you by the
Jesus whom Paul preaches." 14 Also there
were seven sons of Sceva, a Jewish chief
priest, who did so.*

*15 And the evil spirit answered and said,
"Jesus I know, and Paul I know; but who
are you?"*

*16 Then the man in whom the evil spirit was
leaped on them, overpowered them, and
prevailed against them, so that they fled out
of that house naked and wounded. 17 This
became known both to all Jews and Greeks
dwelling in Ephesus; and fear fell on them
all, and the name of the Lord Jesus was
magnified.*

Now I'm not trying to scare you here but you have to understand there is a real war going on between the Kingdom of God and the kingdom of the devil. This is a spiritual war with earthly consequences. Fallen Angels, demons, and demonic possession are all very real things and is not something that the novice should get into with little to no training. One of the best men of God in our age to learn from is Russ Dizdar. His website is www.shatterthedarkness.com for those interested in learning more about his ministry.

We don't need to be scared of the devil but mindful of his ways and unrelenting attacks on our hearts, souls, minds, and bodies.

8 Be sober, be vigilant; because your adversary the devil walks about like a roaring lion, seeking whom he may devour.
9 Resist him, steadfast in the faith, knowing that the same sufferings are experienced by your brotherhood in the world - 1 Peter 5:8-9

[11] lest Satan should take advantage of us; for we are not ignorant of his devices - 2 Cor. 2:11

[7] Therefore submit to God. Resist the devil and he will flee from you. – James 4:7

We don't need to be afraid of what the devil can do to us, we have been given authority over him and all his evil minions. We don't need to even be afraid of being separated from God somehow either here on earth or for all eternity. Let's let the Scriptures speak for themselves, below you can see that nothing can separate us from the love of God in Christ Jesus in addition to Christ giving us all authority to trample on serpents and scorpions and over all the power of the enemy – did you see the word all. That sounds pretty absolute to me. The main thing that we need to realize here is what manner of spirit we are of – 2 Tim 1:7 makes it very clear that God has not given us a spirit of fear, but of power, and of love, and of a sound mind.

*[38] For I am persuaded that neither death
nor life, nor angels nor principalities nor
powers, nor things present nor things to
come, [39] nor height nor depth, nor any
other created thing, shall be able to
separate us from the love of God which is
in Christ Jesus our Lord -Rom. 8:38-39*

*[4] You are of God, little children, and have
overcome them, because He who is in you
is greater than he who is in the world -1
John 4:4*

*[17] Then the seventy returned with joy,
saying, "Lord, even the demons are subject
to us in Your name." [18] And He said to
them, "I saw Satan fall like lightning from
heaven. [19] Behold, I give you the authority
to trample on serpents and scorpions, and
over all the power of the enemy, and
nothing shall by any means hurt you. [20]
Nevertheless do not rejoice in this, that the
spirits are subject to you, but rather rejoice
because your names are written in heaven -
Luke 10: 17-20*

[7] For God has not given us a spirit of fear, but of power and of love and of a sound mind 2 Tim 1:7

[18] There is no fear in love; but perfect love casts out fear, because fear involves torment. But he who fears has not been made perfect in love. 1 John 4:18

Spiritual warfare is very real. Look around you -the social unrest, the violence in our schools and in our streets, the persecution of Christians around the world (including here in the US), and the demoralizing of our society screams spiritual attacks from the devil and his minions. The devil is on the move and making great strides because he knows his time is short - [7] *And war broke out in heaven: Michael and his angels fought with the dragon; and the dragon and his angels fought,* [8] *but they did not prevail, nor was a place found for them in heaven any longer.*

[9] So the great dragon was cast out, that
serpent of old, called the Devil and Satan,
who deceives the whole world; he was cast
to the earth, and his angels were cast out
with him. [10] Then I heard a loud voice saying
in heaven, "Now salvation, and strength,
and the kingdom of our God, and the power
of His Christ have come, for the accuser of
our brethren, who accused them before our
God day and night, has been cast down. [11]
And they overcame him by the blood of the
Lamb and by the word of their testimony,
and they did not love their lives to the death.
[12]Therefore rejoice, O heavens, and you who
dwell in them! ***Woe to the inhabitants of the***
earth and the sea! For the devil has come
down to you, having great wrath, because
he knows that he has a short time.*" Rev.*
12:7-12

But know this: God has already won, He is Victorious. He has already Won the War and those who are in Christ have the Victory – IF They Claim It and Walk in It

Let these verses equip you for the battles to come:

- *For we wrestle not against flesh and blood, but against principalities, against powers, against the rulers of the darkness of this world, against spiritual wickedness in high places. ~Ephesians 6:12*
- *Above all, taking the shield of faith, wherewith ye shall be able to quench all the fiery darts of the wicked. ~Ephesians 6:16*
- *Be sober, be vigilant; because your adversary the devil, as a roaring lion, walketh about, seeking whom he may devour ~1st Peter 5:8*
- *Submit yourselves therefore to God. Resist the devil, and he will flee from you. ~James 4:7*
- *For whatsoever is born of God overcometh the world: and this is the victory that overcometh the world, even our faith. Who is he that overcometh the world, but he that believeth that Jesus is the Son of God? ~1st John 5:4-5*
- *No weapon that is formed against thee shall prosper; and every tongue that shall rise against thee in judgment thou shalt condemn. This is the heritage of the servants of the Lord, and their righteousness is of me, saith the Lord. ~Isaiah 54:17*

The Scriptures above are clear and to the point – we have the authority, we have the victory, we have everything we need to defeat the devil and everything he throws at us if we have the courage and the faith to believe God's Word enough to take action in our daily lives. Will you boldly walk out your faith today?

Praying for your enemies

Let's briefly discuss praying for your enemies. There are several reasons that if you're a follower of Jesus Christ should pray for your enemies. First and foremost we have to guard against hatred and resentment building up within our spirit. Hatred and resentment is like a spiritual cancer that infects our spirit separating us from completing God's perfect will for our life. There is a fundamental Christian principle that Christ taught us and that is to be forgiven we have to forgive others – it's just that simple.

A lot of times when we do not forgive someone, in all reality it's only affecting us - the other person probably has no clue of the entirety of your feelings.

Let's once again look to the Scripture for clarification:

Matt. 5:43-47

43 "You have heard that it was said, 'You shall love your neighbor and hate your enemy.' 44 But I say to you, love your enemies, bless those who curse you, do good to those who hate you, and pray for those who spitefully use you and persecute you, 45 that you may be sons of your Father in heaven; for He makes His sun rise on the evil and on the good, and sends rain on the just and on the unjust. 46 For if you love those who love you, what reward have you? Do not even the tax collectors do the same? 47 And if you greet your brethren only, what do you do more than others? Do not even the tax collectors do so? 48 Therefore you shall be perfect, just as your Father in heaven is perfect.

Rom. 12:9-21

9 Let love be without hypocrisy. Abhor what is evil. Cling to what is good. 10 Be kindly affectionate to one another with brotherly love, in honor giving preference to one another; 11 not lagging in diligence, fervent in spirit, serving the Lord; 12 rejoicing in hope, patient in tribulation, continuing steadfastly in prayer; 13 distributing to the needs of the saints, given to hospitality.

14 Bless those who persecute you; bless and do not curse. 15 Rejoice with those who rejoice, and weep with those who weep. 16 Be of the same mind toward one another. Do not set your mind on high things, but associate with the humble. Do not be wise in your own opinion.

17 Repay no one evil for evil. Have regard for good things in the sight of all men. 18 If it is possible, as much as depends on you, live peaceably with all men. 19 Beloved, do not avenge yourselves, but rather give place to wrath; for it is written, "Vengeance is Mine, I will repay," says the Lord. 20 Therefore

"If your enemy is hungry, feed him;
If he is thirsty, give him a drink;
For in so doing you will heap coals of fire on his head."

[21] ***Do not be overcome by evil, but overcome evil with good.***

Releasing this type of hatred, resentment, and unforgiveness cleanses your spirit as you repent of these things and enables you to draw closer to God. Now this is not to say that there isn't a time and a place for righteous anger. The Bible declares that you can be angry and not sin but you have to be led by the Word of God and His Holy Spirit.

Chapter 11:

Developing Your Prayer List

What is a prayer list?

The simple definition of a prayer list according to yours truly is simply a list of items that you feel compelled to pray for – normally the items on this list are prayed for when I consistent basis every day until God puts it on your heart to move on to something else. For example praying for the salvation of a loved one by their specific name, or if a relative is dealing with a sickness or illness.

Getting Serious!

Developing a prayer list could potentially be one sign that you're starting to take prayer more serious.

It's an indication that you understand the power and the value of praying consistently each and every day to affect change in the dynamics you're dealing with. I found this to be true in my case. Sure I prayed as the Spirit led, or when there was a need but slowly the Holy Spirit put within my heart a burden for the salvation of my mother and other people around me and it was at this point that I started writing down things to pray for and putting it up where I could see it continually. See I'm a visual person and a lot of times if I don't see it I will forget it – I'm sure a lot of you can relate to this, especially with how hectic life can be.

Therefore, I cannot stress strongly enough that once you've created a prayer list that you put it up somewhere in which you will continually see it such as a home office. Oh – make sure you either write it large enough to see it or type it in a font that's large enough for you to see it from a distance.

The bottom line is just to keep it in front of you and in your mind. Don't let prayers go one prayed because of lack of discipline and spiritual laziness. To be a strong Christian prayer warrior requires discipline, vigilance, and the warrior spirit that the Lord himself will mold you into.

They Why

The Why is straightforward here. We all forget things, that's just a reality of life, don't beat yourself up about it just keep it moving ever adapting to changes and situations that the devil attempts to throw at you. As you continue to develop into a prayer warrior your intensity, passion, and desire to serve the living God will increase to the point where you will continually walk victorious – remember you are Christ's ambassadors, the King of Kings and the Lord of lords.

An Example of My Prayer List

In this section I want to share with you my personal prayer list. This is my general list of things that I pray for or about on a consistent basis. Please note the order in which I list them as there is a systematic order in which I pray from the first thing to the last thing (normally).

They are as follows:

- Giving Thanks – showing my appreciation for all that God is doing, has done, and will do
- Repentance - this is something I pray as needed
- Protection - pleading the blood of Jesus over me and my family and those around us
- Salvation - for my family members, neighbors, and specific people my life
- Healing - if there is a specific medical need, but at times I pray that salvation and healing walk hand-in-hand

- Revival - that God would stir the hearts and minds of his people
- Brothers and Sisters in Christ -for protection, healing, leading, for God's perfect will to be done in their lives
- For Leadership in Government - this includes America and Israel
- Workers for the harvest -this is praying the Scriptures -for God to send workers
- Prayer Warriors -for God to raise up Prayer Warriors
- Those Most Vulnerable in Our Society - in this area I pray for the elderly, the sick and affirmed, the homeless and hungry, those in foster care, those still within their mother's womb, and for the children worldwide to be protected. In this section I start to really get into spiritual warfare. I pray against the spiritual forces behind pedophile rings, Satanic networks, human trafficking networks, sex trafficking networks.

I pray that the Lord would send His angels – yes is holy and righteous Angels to protect every single person in our society without a voice who may be being abused, tortured, molested, or maybe they have been kidnapped, and may soon be sacrificed to the enemy. Then ask God specifically to help us and the systematic murder of the children that are still yet in her mother's womb – this Holocaust, this bloodshed has to come to an end if our nation has any chance for redemption. Because understand this this bloodshed is literally part of sacrifices to the devil. Many people don't understand that blood is a currency in the amount of innocent blood that has been shed is overwhelming – help me pray against this brothers and sisters. Through prayer we can shine God's light into the darkness was focus our efforts together in prayer and shine God's light into the darkness to expose this evil and abolish it from our land.

- Against the Enemy - after I've begun to pray for those most vulnerable in our society and against the demonic forces that seek to destroy them I then shift gears and specifically go after the spiritual enemy even more.

Chapter 12:

When It Seems God Doesn't Hear Your Prayers

When God Doesn't Answer Prayers?

We've touched on this already to some degree but let's examine some times in Scripture were men of "Faith" don't have their prayers answered or answered immediately.

- Daniel - Prince of Persia holding him up
- The Disciples of Jesus – Faithless, Perversion, Jesus said, "Because of your unbelief"

- Job - A perfect example of following God faithfully and having sudden destruction fall upon you similar to the way we may pray but not necessarily see an answer to our prayers. God allowed Satan to attack Job and his family – but what you see here is that whatever is happening God is still in charge. Satan had to come and get God's permission to do anything to Job. So even though times may seem dark you are still in the palm of his hand if you faithfully abide in Christ.
- The question you should ask yourself is this – Are you just honoring God with your mouth but your heart is far from Him?

This people draweth nigh unto me with their mouth, and honoureth me with their lips; but their heart is far from me. Matt. 15:8

Dan. 10:12-13

[12] Then said he unto me, Fear not, Daniel:
for from the first day that thou didst set thine
heart to understand, and to chasten thyself
before thy God, thy words were heard, and I
am come for thy words. [13] But the prince of
the kingdom of Persia withstood me one and
twenty days: but, lo, Michael, one of the
chief princes, came to help me; and I
remained there with the kings of Persia.

Matt. 17:15-21

[15] Lord, have mercy on my son: for he is
lunatick, and sore vexed: for ofttimes he
falleth into the fire, and oft into the water. [16]
And I brought him to thy disciples, and they
could not cure him. [17] Then Jesus answered
and said, O faithless and perverse
generation, how long shall I be with you?
how long shall I suffer you? bring him hither
to me.

[18] And Jesus rebuked the devil; and he
departed out of him: and the child was cured
from that very hour. [19] Then came the
disciples to Jesus apart, and said, Why could
not we cast him out? [20] And Jesus said unto
them, Because of your unbelief: for verily I
say unto you, If ye have faith as a grain of
mustard seed, ye shall say unto this
mountain, Remove hence to yonder place;
and it shall remove; and nothing shall be
impossible unto you. [21] Howbeit this kind
goeth not out but by prayer and fasting

Chapter 13:

Fasting and Prayer

If you want to really get serious about prayer than there's no better way than to add fasting to your prayer life. Fasting and prayer can be found throughout both the Old Testament and the New Testament. Fasting and prayer are normally related to drawling close to God and seeking a breakthrough in a particular situation. Let's take a look at some examples of fasting and prayer in the Bible.

Ezra 8: 21-22

21 Then **I proclaimed a fast** there at the
river of Ahava, **that we might humble
ourselves before our God, to seek
from Him the right way for us and our
little ones and all our possessions.** 22
For I was ashamed to request of the king
an escort of soldiers and horsemen to
help us against the enemy on the road,
because we had spoken to the king,
saying, "The hand of our God *is* upon all
those for good who seek Him, but His
power and His wrath *are* against all
those who forsake Him."

In Ezra we can see that the purpose of fasting and praying was to humble their cells before God and to seek God's direction for them and their families. I'm sure many of us can relate to wanting to know what the right path is.

We can see from Scripture that fasting and praying is a way for us to humble ourselves, lean not unto her own understanding, and seek God's direction for our lives. How many of us can truly say that we have done this? Draw close to God and he will draw close to you and you will know your path.

Psalms 35:11-14

11 Fierce witnesses rise up; They ask me
things that I do not know. 12 They reward
me evil for good, *To* the sorrow of my
soul. 13 But as for me, when they were
sick, My clothing *was* sackcloth; I
humbled myself with fasting; And my
prayer would return to my own heart. 14 I
paced about as though *he were* my friend
or brother; I bowed down heavily, as one
who mourns *for his* mother.

In Psalms 35 we again see fasting as a way to humble ourselves before God Almighty. We can also see that prayer comes from the heart. The Scriptures declare, "Out of the abundance of the heart the mouth speaks" – (Matt. 12:34 / Luke 6:45) is a critical spiritual principle or law if you would – for in the power of the tongue there is life and there is death (Proverbs 18:21), speak life! Speak life to your situations, circumstances and call those things that are not as if they are according to the word of God – this is the essence of faith.

- Now **faith <u>is</u> the** substance of things hoped for, **the evidence** of things not seen (Heb. 11:13)
- [6] But without faith it is impossible to please him: for he that cometh to God must believe that he is, and that he is a rewarder of them that diligently seek him (Heb. 11:6).

- [27] And Jesus looking upon them saith, With men it is impossible, but not with God: for with God all things are possible (Mark 10:27)
- [11] Not that I speak in respect of want: for I have learned, in whatsoever state I am, therewith to be content. [12] I know both how to be abased, and I know how to abound: every where and in all things I am instructed both to be full and to be hungry, both to abound and to suffer need. [13] I can do all things through Christ which strengtheneth me (Philippians 4:11-13)

Daniel 9:2-22

2 In the first year of his reign I, Daniel,
understood by the books the number of
the years *specified* by the word of the
Lord through Jeremiah the prophet, that
He would accomplish seventy years in
the desolations of Jerusalem.

3 Then **I set my face toward the Lord**
God to make request by prayer and
supplications, with fasting, sackcloth,
and ashes. 4 And I prayed to the Lord
my God, and made confession, and said,
"O Lord, great and awesome God, who
keeps His covenant and mercy with
those who love Him, and with those who
keep His commandments, 5 we have
sinned and committed iniquity, we have
done wickedly and rebelled, even by
departing from Your precepts and Your
judgments.

[6] Neither have we heeded Your servants
the prophets, who spoke in Your name to
our kings and our princes, to our fathers
and all the people of the land. [7] O Lord,
righteousness *belongs* to You, but to us
shame of face, as *it is* this day—to the
men of Judah, to the inhabitants of
Jerusalem and all Israel, those near and
those far off in all the countries to which
You have driven them, because of the
unfaithfulness which they have
committed against You. [8] "O Lord, to us
belongs shame of face, to our kings, our
princes, and our fathers, because we
have sinned against You. [9] To the Lord
our God *belong* mercy and forgiveness,
though we have rebelled against Him. [10]
We have not obeyed the voice of the
Lord our God, to walk in His laws,
which He set before us by His servants
the prophets.

[11] Yes, all Israel has transgressed Your
law, and has departed so as not to obey
Your voice; therefore the curse and the
oath written in the Law of Moses the
servant of God have been poured out on
us, because we have sinned against Him.
[12] And He has confirmed His words,
which He spoke against us and against
our judges who judged us, by bringing
upon us a great disaster; for under the
whole heaven such has never been done
as what has been done to Jerusalem. [13]
"As *it is* written in the Law of Moses, all
this disaster has come upon us; yet we
have not made our prayer before the
Lord our God, that we might turn from
our iniquities and understand Your truth.
[14] Therefore the Lord has kept the
disaster in mind, and brought it upon us;
for the Lord our God *is* righteous in all
the works which He does, though we
have not obeyed His voice.

[15] And now, O Lord our God, who
brought Your people out of the land of
Egypt with a mighty hand, and made
Yourself a name, as *it is* this day—we
have sinned, we have done wickedly!

[16] O Lord, according to all Your
righteousness, I pray, let Your anger and
Your fury be turned away from Your
city Jerusalem, Your holy mountain;
because for our sins, and for the
iniquities of our fathers, Jerusalem and
Your people *are* a reproach to all *those*
around us. [17] Now therefore, our God,
hear the prayer of Your servant, and his
supplications, and for the Lord's sake
cause Your face to shine on Your
sanctuary, which is desolate.

18 O my God, incline Your ear and hear;
open Your eyes and see our desolations,
and the city which is called by Your
name; for we do not present our
supplications before You because of our
righteous deeds, but because of Your
great mercies. 19 O Lord, hear! O Lord,
forgive! O Lord, listen and act! Do not
delay for Your own sake, my God, for
Your city and Your people are called by
Your name." 20 Now while I *was*
speaking, praying, and confessing my
sin and the sin of my people Israel, and
presenting my supplication before the
Lord my God for the holy mountain of
my God, 21 yes, while I *was* speaking in
prayer, the man Gabriel, whom I had
seen in the vision at the beginning, being
caused to fly swiftly, reached me about
the time of the evening offering. 22 And
he informed *me,* and talked with me, and
said, "O Daniel, I have now come forth
to give you skill to understand.

The Scripture in Daniel 9 is a great example of how to pray for your country. Though God was talking specifically to Solomon regarding the house of the Lord we can see from Daniel chapter 9 that Daniel still prayed according to 2 Chon. 7:14. I'm sure a lot of you reading this book probably know the Scripture by heart but how many of us have fasted and prayed like Daniel to seek a healing for the land. Understand to heal the land requires that each of us are healed ourselves internally and spiritually.

- [14] If my people, which are called by my name, shall humble themselves, and pray, and seek my face, and turn from their wicked ways; then will I hear from heaven, and will forgive their sin, and will heal their land - (2 Chron. 7:14).

Matthew 17:20-21 Mark 9:28-29

[20] And Jesus said unto them, Because of
your unbelief: for verily I say unto you,
If ye have faith as a grain of mustard
seed, ye shall say unto this mountain,
Remove hence to yonder place; and it
shall remove; and nothing shall be
impossible unto you. [21] Howbeit this
kind goeth not out but by prayer and
fasting.

As we can see without faith you will have no victory in spiritual warfare. And remember, without faith it is impossible to please God – the One who enlisted you in His army. But make no mistake about it we will endure hardship as a good soldier of Jesus Christ according to Scripture –(2 Tim 2:3).

However, hardship is not defeat it is just merely part of the war that were all in and some battles leave us more wounded than others. Nevertheless we have the victory in Christ regardless of how wounded we get.

Having the proper mindset is critical and this mindset comes from transforming yourself into the word of God, not the Word of God transforming itself into today's societal norms. Remember, heaven and earth will pass away but God's Word will remain the same – (Matt. 24:35).

It's important that we don't get discouraged in the battle, going back to the mindset once again.

Could you imagine the confusion of the apostles had when they attempted to invoke the name of Jesus and the demon wasn't cast out? Why did this happen? Jesus says this happen because of two things – their unbelief and the fact that this particular type of demon only comes out through fasting and prayer. I would speculate that because of the fierceness of this particular demon, because the apostles believe the lie of the physical world, of what they saw they were moved in their heart to believe that this demon is too strong. I believe this is the essence of where their unbelief stemmed from.

Now this is just speculation based off of reading the Scriptures no one can be entirely sure where of their unbelief stemmed from but it did originate from somewhere.

Additionally Jesus indicated that this particular type of demon only comes out through fasting and prayer. Now was He specifically talking regarding the apostles because of their unbelief or can this be universally applied? I tend to look at it like this – because of the apostles unbelief they needed to humble themselves before God by fasting and then pray for the demon to be removed. Because the Scriptures very clearly tell us that Christ has given us all authority over the enemy.

Let's review this real quick:

- Then He called His twelve disciples together and gave them power and authority over **all demons**, and to cure diseases. [2] He sent them to preach the kingdom of God and to heal the sick - (Luke 9:1-2)

- [18] And He said to them, "I saw Satan fall like lightning from heaven. [19] Behold, I give you the authority to trample on serpents and scorpions, **<u>and over all the power of the enemy</u>**, and nothing shall by any means hurt you. [20] Nevertheless do not rejoice in this, that the spirits are subject to you, but rather rejoice because your names are written in heaven." – (Luke 10:18-20).

The main thing to remember about the Scripture is to have faith, real faith and if you're struggling with faith pray and ask God to give you the faith that's needed to do his will each and every day. It's not just enough to know about God or to even read a book about God – you have to believe in your hearts and then confessed publicly with your mouth - (Rom 10:9-10).

Strongholds of the enemy may be present in your life or in a situation during which time is highly recommended if you want to have the victory over these things that you fast and pray.

Luke 2:36-38

36 And there was one Anna, a prophetess, the daughter of Phanuel, of the tribe of Aser: she was of a great age, and had lived with an husband seven years from her virginity; 37 And she was a widow of about fourscore and four years, which departed not from the temple, but served God with fastings and prayers night and day. 38 And she coming in that instant gave thanks likewise unto the Lord, and spake of him to all them that looked for redemption in Jerusalem.

Here we see a combination of a virtuous woman and a prayer warrior. The Scriptures indicate that she was a woman of honor who followed the word of God even after her husband's death. We can see her dedication to the Lord in the fact that she did not depart from the temple but served God with fastings and prayers both day and night all the meanwhile continuingly telling people where they can find redemption – a powerful woman of God.

Luke 5:33-35

33 And they said unto him, Why do the
disciples of John fast often, and make
prayers, and likewise the disciples of the
Pharisees; but thine eat and drink? 34
And he said unto them, Can ye make the
children of the bridechamber fast, while
the bridegroom is with them? 35 **But the
days will come, when the bridegroom
shall be taken away from them, and
then shall they fast in those days.**

Brothers and sisters we are in the days Jesus spoke about, the days in which we shall fast and pray. When is the last time you fasted and prayed? If you're truly serious about being a prayer warrior, if you want to take your prayer life to the next level, if you want to draw close to God than it's time to start fasting and praying on a more regular basis.

Now obviously if you have specific medical needs or conditions it's important to consult with your primary doctor to ensure that it is safe for you to fast. If you do have medical conditions that preclude you from completely fasting then maybe consider a juice fast. A juice fast requires the use of a juicer that processes vegetables and fruits into pure juice without the pulp and the fiber.

This is a great way to get started with fasting because not only are you fasting from particular items that you would normally eat but you're also doing something that will promote the overall health and well-being of your body – the temple of the living God.

1 Cor 7:2-5

2 Nevertheless, to avoid fornication, let
every man have his own wife, and let
every woman have her own husband. 3
Let the husband render unto the wife due
benevolence: and likewise also the wife
unto the husband. 4 The wife hath not
power of her own body, but the husband:
and likewise also the husband hath not
power of his own body, but the wife. 5
**Defraud ye not one the other, except it
be with consent for a time, that ye
may give yourselves to fasting and
prayer;** and come together again, that
Satan tempt you not for your
incontinency.

The above Scripture is very interesting when we understand that the two become one in the flesh (Matt.19:5 / Mark 10:8 / 1 Cor. 6:16 / Eph. 5:31). However, the fact that the two become one in the flesh does not mean they come together as one in the spirit. Though the two are one in the flesh it is clear that each one has to work out our own salvation with fear and trembling before the Lord – (Philippians 2:12)

Scripture indicates not to withhold the love that is due one another except with consent for a time that you may give yourself to fasting and prayer and then come together again. There are some key points that we should address here:

- First and foremost there needs to be permission given – an agreement prior to restraining from giving yourself to one another.

- Secondly there is a time that is indicated in the agreement whether it's a day a week, whatever it is it is verbally articulated and agreed to by both parties.
- The only time this is permitted is for fasting and prayer
- You must come together immediately following your fast and prayer to ensure you are not tempted.

Chapter 14: Conclusion

It's up to each one of us to actively get into the fight, or maybe more importantly realize there is a war going on spiritually and we are all in a battle for our very souls. For the scriptures declare to "Wherefore, my beloved, as ye have always obeyed, not as in my presence only, but now much more in my absence, work out your own salvation with fear and trembling - Philippians 2:12"

This is a real war in the Spiritual realm that continues to bleed over into the physical world. So many men and women of God aren't even in the fight because they refuse to address their sin and run to God for forgiveness, let me tell you now – "As long as there is breath in Your lungs there is Hope in God for Change" – AJF

We must all do what we can, when we can, as God enables us . . . From personally getting right with God, to effectively leading, guiding and protecting your family, to even effecting your community, society, and ultimately the world. Christians have forgotten what the "Far Left" has not – That one person can make a difference in the world and united we become stronger.

Why have Christians forgotten this critical lesson from History – Do we not remember that 12 men (Christ and the 11 Apostles – I don't really count Judas) Changed the World. We as Christian need to walk in that same boldness that they have walked in, that same Spirit of Conviction, Compassion, and Love. There is a time for everything under heaven and as you draw close to Jesus Christ the Holy Spirit will continually lead and guide you. The Question is do you really have Faith –

If you really have Faith you will "Take Action for the Kingdom of God". I challenge you to examine if you are in fact in the faith and to walk courageously, yes boldly in the Word of God for His name's sake. If we want to all make America great again then it's going to have to start with a transformation of each of our hearts and the hearts of those that claim to follow Christ – and that starts with Prayer.

What does the Scriptures say, "If my people, which are called by my name, shall **humble themselves, and Pray**, and seek my face, and turn from their wicked ways; then will I hear from heaven, and will forgive their sin, and will heal their land. 2 Chronicles 7:14" The time is now – "Take Action for the Kingdom of God" and get about the Father's business for tomorrow is never promised.

"Think For Yourself and Learn

Directly From God"

If you've learned nothing else in reading this book you've learned that without prayer our spiritual lives are basically non-existent. We cannot know God if we do not speak to Him and listen to Him. We cannot speak or listen to Him if we do not pray. There is a major difference between knowing God and being known by God.

Before I end this I also want to leave you with this scriptural truth: God hears and answers each and every prayer we say. Silent or out loud. Big or small concerns. He hears and answers them all. His answers may not always be what we want, but they will always be what we need

God bless each and every one of you who have read this book - know that I pray for all You as my Brother or Sister in Christ and that you are Not Alone in the War and together we can make a difference.

Special Gift

God has a Gift for You!   The Plan of Salvation:

There is no formal prayer of salvation as many churches would have you believe, God's Word is very clear - there is only one way to get to the Father in heaven and that is through Jesus Christ (John 14:6). Jesus says that you must be born again to enter into heaven (John 3:3-5).

Salvation is simply the first step in building an open and honest relationship with God. We all have sinned and fall short every day, but there is Hope in Jesus Christ - Just cry out to God in sincerity and honesty asking for forgiveness and for Him to Save you, Sanctify you, and fill you with His Holy Spirit - Ask for His will to be done in your life on earth as it is in Heaven and That's it, now just keep it real with God.

A Warning:

The Christian walk is not an easy life on the surface. The Word of God says that we will be hated in all the world for Christ namesake (Matt. 24:9). The Bible says that in the last days are enemy prevail against us physically until Christ returns to save us (Dan 7:21, 22). Furthermore, we must endure hardship as a good soldier of Jesus Christ (2 Tim 2:3) and yet we are never alone in this, God promises us that He will never leave us nor forsake us if we believe in him (Matt.28:20).

In everything we go through we have the peace and joy of God which surpasses all understanding (Philp. 4:6-8) The Bible declares, "For I consider the sufferings of this present time are not worthy to be compared with the glory which shall be revealed in us". (Rom 8:18). However, in all these things we are more than conquerors through Jesus Christ (Rom. 8:37)

Stay In Contact

Our Contact Information

Stay in Contact with the American Christian Defense Alliance, Inc.
Contactus@acdainc.org Or Email Us Though Our Website At:
www.ACDAInc.Org

Join Our Mailing List

We also Greatly Appreciate You Signing Up For Our Mailing List and Providing a Good Rating and review for this Book. Your reviews help other people like yourself find this book on Amazon and benefit from its contents.

If You or Your Family have been Blessed by this book please let us know by dropping us a line through our website at http://acdainc.org

Find All Our Books

<u>Our Books on Amazon</u>:

Parenting: How To Be A Great Parent And Raise Awesome Kids

Real Men Don't Make Promises: Understanding Oaths, Pacts, Covenants & Promises From A Biblical Perspective

Salvation for Your Unsaved Mom: 10 Things to Tell Your Mom Before She Dies

The Perfection of Purity: A Message To My Daughter

A Vague Notion: How To Overcome Limiting Beliefs of Fear and Anxiety Through the Word of God

Biblical Bug Out: Don't Bug In - Follow The Calling

Christian Prepping 101: How To Start Prepping

Martial Arts Ministry: How To Start A Martial Arts Ministry

Bible Studies for Belts: A Guide for Christian Martial Arts, Vol. 1: White Belt

Prepping: Survival Basics

How to Finance Your Full-Time RV Dream

Made in the USA
Las Vegas, NV
08 February 2025

17743280R00088